My Note for You:

TO ALL SOON TO BE EMPTY NESTERS
(AND MY FUTURE SELF)

LETTING GO
Published by LHC Publishing 2021

Printed in the USA.

All inquiries should be directed to
www.LHCpublishing.com

ISBN-13: 978-1-952517-02-0 Paperback
ISBN-13: 978-1-952517-03-7 Hardcover

Life's Biggest Moments
LETTING GO

For The Soon-To-Be Empty Nester

WRITTEN BY
EEVI JONES

Take Heart, My Love:

Time has come for this little bird
to spread her mighty wings.
To discover and explore her own self,
for today, her new future begins.

So you watch her excitedly packing,
see her waving and smile a big smile.
Driving off, toward a life of her own,
not coming back home for a while.

"Time moves fast," they'd say.
But you thought it all a lie.
Until you saw years rushing by
in the blink of your own eye.

From baby teeth, first steps,
recitals, games, and more;
to tumbling over her piles of shoes
spread across the floor.

First dances, boyfriends, girlfriends;
first falls, successes, tears.
First everythings! You fought your way
through long days, yet such short years.

No one prepared you for the changes
she'd bring into your life.
Countless worries, doubts, lost sleep,
the tears you may have cried.

Yet her happiness, her wins,
her joy in life repaid
tenfold-a-thousand-million
of sacrifices made.

Embracing her and kissing her.
Skipping, holding hands.
Puddle-jumps and pies of mud,
castles built in sand.

Reading books, cuddles and play,
spending time together.
But still you ask: "What could I have done?
Sooner? Longer? Better?"

So you wish you could stop time.
Just for a little while.
Just long enough to undo wrongs,
when tears replaced her smile.

When doubts filled every minute.
When doubts filled every day.
When you believed to be unfit
to *adult*, to lead the way.

Afraid to fail and plunder,
to mess up, to botch, to break.
Yet we all had to gradually grow
and learn by trial and mistake.

NO ONE knows what they're doing,
for there's no playbook, key, or guide.
Making it up, inventing new rules,
we all stumble our way through life.

We're all learning along the way,
so give yourself some grace.
For by giving your very best every day,
a beautiful human you've raised.

Early Christmas mornings,
sparkling eyes beneath the tree,
Tooth Fairies and Leprechauns –
all crafted make-believe.

Forevermore remembered
are those moments you both hold.
Vacations, giggles, holidays –
treasured memories of gold.

You taught her, and she taught you
'bout life – the easy and the rough.
You ingrained compassion and care.
She instilled in you unconditional love.

Raising her, preparing her.
This string of moments giving rise
to the most important, most wondrous task
you've ever performed in your life.

First days and last days, you had plenty of those.
Yet you didn't have nearly enough.
Holding her tightly, your heart swells with pride.
With fierceness you share your unending love.

Letting go may be hard.
Letting go may be tough.
Yet know that whatever you gave
was more than enough!

Driving off toward a fate of her own,
she cannot wait to see what life brings.
For with your steadfast, unconditional love
she's prepared to spread her beautiful wings.

The bird has left its nest,
the butterfly its cocoon.
Yet with a heavy but happy heart you know
she'll be back home for her first visit soon.

ABOUT THE AUTHOR

Writing under a number of pen names, Eevi Jones is a USA Today & WSJ bestselling and award-winning author and ghostwriter of children's books.

Born in former East Germany to a German mother and a Vietnamese father, Eevi loves to infuse her children's books with racial diversity. Always drawing inspiration from her own two children, she writes about unique interests and aspires to find fun and exciting ways to have kids discover and learn about the magnificent marvels this world has to offer.

Eevi has been featured in Forbes, Scary Mommy, Business Insider, Huffington Post, Exceptional Parent Magazine, and more.

She can be found online at www.BravingTheWorldBooks.com.

A WORD BY THE AUTHOR

Yesterday, my boys took their first steps. Today they're getting ready to conquer the world. First days and last days, we've had plenty of those. Yet we didn't have nearly enough. I hope that with this book you come to see that whatever you gave was more than enough. What a magnificent being you have raised.

If you enjoyed this book, it would mean the world to me if you would take a short minute to leave a heartfelt review. Thank you.

OTHER WORKS BY THIS AUTHOR

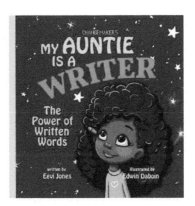

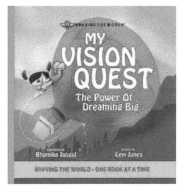

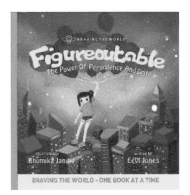

... AND MANY MORE

EMPTY NESTER - RESOURCES

Whatever you are currently feeling, please know that you're NOT alone.

Below, I've provided a link to a number of wonderful resources and Facebook communities that are specifically for those who need support during this time of their lives. A lot of parents go through ENS (Empty-Nest-Syndrome). It can be a very lonely experience, and having someone to share your thoughts and feelings with can help us go through the process.

http://www.bravingtheworldbooks.com/empty-nester-resources

CPSIA information can be obtained
at www.ICGtesting.com
Printed in the USA
BVHW020442210821
614851BV00006B/521

9 781952 517037